# The Ottoman Empire

## The History of the Turkish Empire that Lasted Over 600 Years

# Table of Contents

Introduction ................................................................... 1

Chapter One: The Founding ......................................... 5

Chapter Two: The Rise ................................................. 14

Chapter Three: The Reign of the Conqueror ............. 24

Chapter Four: The Saint in the Shadows ..................... 35

Chapter Five: The Zenith of the Empire
                   and the Sword of the Grim ................... 45

Chapter Six: The Reign of the Magnificent ................ 56

Chapter Seven: The Dissolution ................................... 68

Chapter Eight: The Decline and the Fall ..................... 75

Conclusion ................................................................... 85

# Introduction

When you think of the word "Ottoman," the first image that probably comes to mind is low, overstuffed yet versatile pieces of upholstery, isn't it? What if I told you that your thoughts are only 50% right? What if I told you that the word "Ottoman" goes beyond stunning pieces of reception room furniture to a powerful western Turkish dynasty that existed long ago in the thirteenth century?

The name "Ottoman" was coined from the chieftain (or "Bey") called Osman, who declared independence from the Seljuk Turks. This beautiful book takes you through the captivating rise and fall of the powerful Ottoman dynasty, from its origins to its inception as a world power that served as a turning point in the history of North Africa, Southeast Europe, the Middle East, and even the rest of the world.

For a period spanning over five centuries, this empire had a vast and powerful stronghold, expanding from a tiny obscure patch in western Anatolia in the year 1290 to become a force to reckon with. It became one of the most extensive yet most influential empires the world has ever known.

The size was not the only asset the Ottomans had. The empire was a melting pot of linguistic, religious, and ethnic circles, including but not limited to the Albanians, Armenians, Bulgarians, Bosnians, Greeks, Hungarians, Jews, Kurds, Serbs, and Turks, each with their own culture, traditions, values, language, and unique history.

A lot of documentation exists about this dynasty, but I am confident in this text's ability to take you on a virtual tour through the other side of the Orient. Here, you will find the ideas behind the founding of this vast empire, its dissolution, and its decline. You will also discover the notable accomplishments of some of its greatest sultans, all of whom were descendants of Osman's house.

We'll go over the achievements of the greatest three sultans, the first of whom is Mehmed II (1444-1481), the conqueror of Constantinople, who single-handedly led his troops to end the thousand-year-long reign of the Byzantine Empire. Trust me when I say this Sultan has more titles than any influential figure in the Game of Thrones franchise.

Another sultan in the hall of fame is Selim I (1512-1520), who set the stage for the pinnacle of Ottoman authority for his son Süleyman (1521-1566), another sultan worthy of note who conquered Belgrade and Budapest. He was also responsible for reforming Ottoman laws that allowed the empire's legislation to adapt to its continuous expansion.

Is your interest piqued yet? Are you picking role models already? If you are, then you might be jumping the gun. This book is not your usual boring historical literature. I can bet you a dollar (or ten) that no page will make you fall asleep. The fall of the empire, though saddening, brings to light the much-needed reforms brought about by the independence granted to all Ottoman states. Not a fan of spoilers? That's okay. I suggest you find a chair, kick back and enjoy some good old Ottoman politics.

# Chapter One:

## The Founding

The origin of the Ottoman dynasty is shrouded in secrecy and a bit of mystery. Osman, the first, a Seljuk Turk, the son of Ertuğrul of Eskişehir (now West Central Turkey), was born in the year 1258 CE. He was born in the city of Söğüt, of Bithynia's northwestern Anatolian region. He is the founder of the Ottoman Empire. The alternate spellings for the name Osman are Othman, Ottman, or Uthman (in Arabic). This name is the origin of the word "Ottoman."

The story of the Ottoman empire begins with the Turkish speaking nomads from parts of outer Mongolia and Central Asia. They migrated to Asia Minor, Iranian plateaus, and Transoxiana (modern-day Uzbekistan). Sometime in the 10th century, due to limited grazing areas, food scarcity, and immense pressure from surrounding tribes, they were forced to find new trade opportunities and greener pastures. These Turkic nomads, under the aegis of the Seljuks, crossed the Amu Darya, entering Transoxiana of northeastern Iran. The Ghaznavid Empire at the time ruled these parts. The Seljuks defeated the Ghaznavid force at the fortress of Dandanqan between Sarakhs (North-East Iran) and Marv (present-day Turkmenistan).

The downfall of the Ghaznavid army automatically made the Seljuks the rulers of North-Eastern Iran under the leadership of their chief, Rukn al-dunya wa al-Din Abu Talib Muhammad Toghrul-Beg ibn Mikail, also known as Tughril or Toghrïl Beg. He was born 990 AD and ruled from 1037-1063.

Tughril captured Ray (modern-day Tehran) and made it his capital. Following his death on September 4, 1063, his 22-year-old nephew, Alp Arsalan (1064-1072), was crowned the new Sultan, owning the caliph's supremacy as Islam's supreme religious commander. Alp Arsalan fulfilled his uncle's dream of completely subduing Iran and consolidating the Seljuk laws in the southern Caucasus.

The Seljuk army led by Alp Arsalan conquered the Greek Byzantine territory in a battle fought on August 12, 1071, in Manzikert north of Lake Van. For the first time in historical literature, Emperor Romanus Diogenes (Emperor Romanus IV), a Byzantine ruler, was captured by a Muslim ruler as a prisoner of war. It is safe to assume that the Byzantine state never recovered from that insult.

The Islamization of Anatolia increased with the arrival of the Mongols under the command of Ghengis Khan, their ruler at the time who seized the Middle East and Central Asia in 1220, putting to death more than half of the civilian populace and committing the other half into slavery or a life of captivity. Many of these slaves died of sickness, hunger, or both. To survive, they had to eat cats, dogs, and even each other for an entire year as Ghengis Khan's men had set all the granaries and food stores on fire.

As Mongol armies kept wreaking havoc in parts of Khorasan and Central Asia, fugitives fled to seek asylum in Anatolia. Following the Mongol invasion and the defeat of the Seljuks, more refugees, including manufacturers, artisans, scholars, and merchants, landed in the western region of Anatolia, bringing their talent and know-how.

Osman's ancestors were of the Qayi tribe who entered Anatolia with a significant number of Turk Oğuz nomads who, after migration from central Asia, entrenched themselves in the Seljuk dynasty of Mesopotamia and Iran in the middle of the 11th century. Following the death of the Seljuk sultanate of Rum, Anatolia underwent segregation into a mishmash of independent states known as Anatolian Bey links. Following the Mongol Empire's hostile takeover, one of the independent Turk dynasties led by Osman, the first compelled by the direct military rule of eastern Anatolia, arose.

Osman was not always the fierce warrior we all know and read about in books. The young Osman, according to legend, was praised widely for his devotion and spiritual lifestyle. He stayed at the home of Sheikh Edebali from 1206-1326. To Osman, the sheik was a mentor and teacher in all things spiritual and holy. One night, at the Edebali's home, he had a vision of a prosperous empire ruled by him and his offspring. This vision is known as Osman's dream, which was only made public about 100 years after Osman's death and was said to be the inspiration for the conquests leading to the founding of the Ottoman Empire.

In his dream, Osman saw a large tree (representing the empire) with links to the roots of the four major rivers — the Danube, Tigris, Nile, and Euphrates. This tree also shaded the major mountain ranges — the Atlas, Caucasus, Balkans, and Taurus. The crescent moon shone on all the summits of the mountains, the muezzin call to prayer sounding from their galleries mixed with the resonant voices of a thousand nightingales and every other singing bird. Suddenly, a mighty gust of wind turned towards Constantinople, a city at the junction of two continents and two oceans reminiscent of a diamond between two emeralds and two sapphires.

In this dream, Osman was about to place the priceless jewel on his finger when he awoke. Osman narrated his vision to the sheik with such clarity that the sheik was, without a doubt, convinced that glory, prosperity, and power lingered in Osman's future. Edebali was so pleased that he gave his daughter Mal Hatun to Osman as a wife, a union he vehemently opposed due to a disparity in social status and position.

It is common knowledge that Osman, the first, founder of the Ottoman Empire, began as a Gâzi (a warrior for Islam). As a frontier commander, he waged holy wars on the Byzantine country from his small settlement in the district of Söğüt in western Anatolia (now a neighborhood in Bilecik Province, Turkey).

Undertaking holy wars (Gazâ) against infidels allowed him to build a solid reputation as a devout Muslim ruler seeking to expand Islamic territory (Dar Ul-Islam). He accomplished this at the price of the Christian rulers of Europe and the Byzantine Empire, which represented realms of war (Dar Ul-Harb). He not only declared religious wars but also launched raids (Akin) against non-Muslims. These raids provided worldly motivation and profitable gain, helping them accumulate trophies and slaves and serve as frontline armies raiding enemy territory, spreading fear in the hearts of the inhabitants of towns about to be captured.

A formal system of governance was created under Osman's rule. This system changed the game for the Ottoman Empire. It made use of legal entities known as "millets" under which various religious and ethnic minority groups had the power to manage their affairs with considerable leeway and independence from the central monarchy.

Osman moved the borders of the Ottoman settlements to the Byzantine dynasty's edge and, through his son Orhan, claimed Bursa as capital, setting the pace for the early political and economic development of the nation. He was fondly called "Kara," which means black in modern Turkish, and courageous or brave in ancient Turkish. Osman's bravery is the reason for the age-old Turkish phrase "May he be as good as Osman." This phrase was carved into Osman's epitaph in a tomb overlooking the sea towards Constantinople. His crypt, together with the grave of his predecessors, became a center for Islamic pilgrimage and is still a tourist hot spot. The age-old phrase inscribed on Osman's epitaph is both a blessing and a prayer, uttered through centuries by successors to the throne to honor the man who, by divine law, created a world subduing power from a single tribe.

After Osman's death, Orhan, the younger of the dead Sultan's two sons, was named successor to the throne based on his military might and achievements. Orhan's elder brother, Ala-ed-din Pasha, was more scholarly, devoting his entire life to the pursuit of knowledge, the law's learning, and spiritual devotion. Ala-ed-din was a Faqih (an expert in Islamic law). Orhan appointed him as "Grand Vizier," a post which handled day to day administration of all matters related to the empire, other pending issues of state, organization of the cavalry and military forces, and the drafting of the legislature.

In some accounts, Ala-ed-din Pasha is the elder brother of Orhan. Other reports claim that even though Sultan Orhan Gazi has an elder brother with the same name, he is not to be confused with the vizier. During Orhan's rule, the "Akçe," a Turkish coin was minted in his name. His nickname "Gâzi" stemmed from the fact that, like his father, he fought many holy wars in his lifetime. However, this did not stop him from sharing a considerable portion of his wealth with the poor.

Sultan Orhan Gazi spent time in the company of the commoners listening to their thoughts and complaints. He married a Byzantine noblewoman named Holofira, who, after conversion to Islam, became Nilufer Hatun. Murad Hüdavendigar (Murad I), the next Sultan, was a product of that marriage. Apart from capturing Bursa as capital, the Sultan took over Iznik (Nicea) in 1330, Mudurnu, in 1331, Gemlik, in 1333. In 1337 he took over Izmit, and then in 1354, he took over Ankara and Gallipoli-Dardanelles. These victories played a large part in extending the Ottoman Empire all the way to the Bosphorus' Asian shores in 1352, as well as Thrace.

# Chapter Two:

## The Rise

In 1354, the Ottomans invaded Europe and made their mark on the Gallipoli Peninsula while conquering Ankara on the dry, humid Anatolian plains. With the death of the Serbian ruler Stefan Dušan (fondly called Stefan Uroš IV in 1355) and the Serbian Empire's dissolution, the Ottomans seized the opportunity to invade the Balkans and take for themselves the town of Adrianople in 1361. The third Sultan of the Ottoman Empire, Sultan Murad I (1362-1389) declared war against southern Bulgaria and Thrace.

In response, the Pope declared battle, which urged the Serbs to take up a united front in conjunction with all Orthodox Christian rulers. In the face of such strong resistance, Murad I gained an impressive victory on the Maritsa river in the year 1371, capturing Macedonia, Bulgaria, and southern Serbia. In 1385, they took over Sofia (farther into Bulgaria) and usurped Nish. Two years later, in 1387, they conquered Thessaloniki (modern-day northern Greece).

After this, Murad declared war on the Balkan states, who had merged with the Serbian prince Lazar. The Ottomans defeated the Christian alliance in the field of the blackbirds (Kosovo-polje), where both leaders (Murad I and Lazar) lost their lives. The new Sultan, Bayezid I (1389-1402), continued the fight against the Balkans, and in the east, Bayezid took over Karaman (southwest Anatolia) from the year 1396-1397. The Ottoman expansion continued swiftly until the capture of the Vidin principality, after which Bayezid seized the towns of Albistan and Malatya in the Euphrates in 1399.

During this period, Timur, the conqueror (Timur meaning "iron" in Turkic), a Turko-Mongol, and the founder of the Timurid Empire of Persia and Central Asia, had made a name for himself creating an empire so vast it covered central Asia, Iran, and India. In 1400-1401, Timur moved his army towards Anatolia, declaring a visible challenge to the Sultan of the Ottoman Empire. Angry at Timur's bullying and use of insulting language, Sultan Bayezid I charged eastward to attack Timur.

Ankara's great battle occurred in July 1402 at Ankara, where Timur brought the Ottomans to their knees, capturing Sultan Bayezid and his two sons Süleyman and Mehmed. This battle is of considerable significance in history as it was the only time a sultan was captured in person as a prisoner of war. The capture of the Sultan almost led to the extinction of the Ottoman Empire. However, Timur, who was widely known as Timur, the diplomat, did not see it fit to destroy the Ottoman state. To him, it did not bode well to crush a Muslim nation who had pledged their life to fight infidels at the time. Timur only insisted on obedience from the Ottomans (which he got for a couple of decades at least) and treated Sultan Bayezid not as a captive but as a guest. Sultan Bayezid I ended his disgrace of living as a captive of war with his death in Akşehir on March 8 1403. Timur decided to give Bayezid's sons small domains in the Balkans and Anatolia so they would do battle among themselves to gain independence over the little left of their father's empire. This period was known as the Ottoman interregnum or Fetret Devri (in Turkish), which lasted from 1402- 1413.

Timur himself marched to the Mediterranean shores seizing Smyrna (a Greek city on the Aegean coast of Anatolia) in December 1402. Smyrna (modern-day Izmir) rose to prominence due to its strategic location as a port. It was a great inland connection that was easy to defend. He made his way back to central Asia, where he died preparing for his Chinese invasion in the year 1405.

At first, the war for Bayezid's throne centered on Isa in Bursa and Balikersir, Mehmed in Amasya, and Süleyman in Edirne (northwest Turkey). Of the three, Süleyman was the most powerful contender for the throne, considering his achievements in Edirne, and the use of his father's Islamic warriors (Gâzi) and cavalry, all of which remained intact. He cemented his position further with the countless peace treaties he signed with the Christian leaders of Europe. He did this to gain the financial support and political favor of the Serbian nations and the Byzantine state. His master plan was to affiliate his command in southeastern Europe and use it as a prop to ambush Anatolia with the backing of his new Christian "friends."

His brothers Mehmed and Isa viewed him as a significant menace to their administration. After 11 years of civil war and strife, neither Musa, Süleyman, nor Isa emerged heir to the Ottoman throne; instead Mehmed, ruler of Amasya in northern Anatolia, became the new Sultan of the Ottoman state. Mehmed I (1413- 1421) and his heir Murad II (1421-1444; 1446- 1451) devoted their time to subduing internal insurgence coordinated by members of the Ottoman empire and reinstating authority of the central government. They did this by overpowering all Turcoman supremacies that had reclaimed sovereignty under Timur.

As the newly reinstated Sultan of the Ottoman Empire, Mehmed dismissed the controversial religious ruler Sheik Bedreddin (Sımavna Kadısıoğlu Şeyh Bedreddin), theologian, mystic, jurist, and revolutionary, whose leadership led to a large-scale uprising and a revolt in 1416 against the Ottoman Empire. Mehmed also dismissed the Gâzi leaders supporting his brother Musa, deporting them to Anatolia and returning Salonica and Byzantine lands surrounding Constantinople to Manuel, the Byzantine emperor at the time.

To restore the authority of the noble Ottoman families, he signed peace treaties with Venice and Genoa, seizing the opportunity to rebuild his army before plunging headfirst into military warfare. He wanted to avoid misinterpretation of his modus operandi as a sign of weakness, especially among the leaders of the Turkish beylinks in Anatolia, who had done nothing other than profit from Bayezid's death. So, to show them who was boss, he decided to attack the Turkoman countries of western and southwestern Anatolia, taking back most of the possessions Murad and Bayezid had looted from Karaman, which Timur had rightfully handed over to them following the battle of Ankara.

Musa, Mehmed's brother, made Bedreddin his "Qadi" or supreme judge of his army, leading to a powerful rebellion against Mehmed's authority and several sects of the empire. The capture of Sheik Bedreddin by Mehmed's grand vizier, Bayezid Pasha, was the result of a 4-year-long war. Bedreddin was hanged in Serres, a city in modern-day Greece, in 1420.

Mehmed died in 1421 and was buried in a mausoleum in Bursa near a mosque he built. This was called the green mosque on account of its beautifully decorated glazed green tiles. After this, Murad II, the great son of Mehmed II, born June 16, 1404, with the title Gazavât-ı Sultan Murad, ascended the throne at the age of 16. Murad II's reign was one of the most captivating in Ottoman history. The Sultan was a man of science and learning who was opposed to war and bloodshed. He preferred the mystic arts and poetry and portrayed himself as a simple soldier who took no joy in royal extravagance. He painted himself as a noble ghâzi ruler seeking to unify Muslim rule against the Hungarians, Venetians, and other non-Muslims.

This pretty picture he painted to the public gained him the support of the entire Muslim nation beyond the Ottoman territories, not just for himself but for his substantial and lavish campaigns. Murad's public image won him the favor of the Mamālīk and Muslim Delhi sultanate of India, representing the larger Muslim population of the Dar-al-Islam. He was notably famous for being the ghâzi king who went to war against "Caffres" (a derogatory term for non-Muslims) and served as the defender and leader of the lesser ghâzi.

Under Murad II, the Ottomans continued their procession westward into the heart of the Balkans. Once more, the battle line was drawn, this time under Vladislaus III of Varna (1434-1444) king of Poland and Hungary, the Serbians under the leadership of Đurađ (George) Branković, and the overall leader of the anti-Ottoman confederacy John Hunyadi, the governor of Transylvania. These three united against the Ottomans and later suffered defeat at Varna in 1444 following King Vladislaus' death on the battlefield. The Ottoman victory at the battle of Varna led to the Christian forces ending their efforts to stop the Ottomans from invading the Balkans.

In 1444, Murad II abdicated his throne in favor of his 12-year-old son Mehmed II the conqueror. His abdication caused a power struggle in the Ottoman Empire between his grand vizier Çandarlı Halil Pasha, the new Sultan Mehmed's personal tutor Zoganos, and Şihâbeddin the Beylerbey (literally translated to "the commander of commanders") of Rūm-ėli. Murad II returned to the throne after pleas from his grand vizier Çandarlı Halil Pasha because of a mutiny led by the Janissaries — elite foot soldiers making up the majority of the Ottoman sultans' household bodyguards and troops. During Murad II's second reign, Mehmet II retained the title of the Sultan but only acted as a governor of Manisa.

These Janissaries drafted following the Devşirme system of tribute, which forcefully recruited soldiers from the young children of Balkan Christian subjects, consisted of Albanians, Bosnians, Serbs, Bulgarians, Croats, and Greeks. Murad II handled the mutiny, declaring war on and defeating the Christian army at the second battle of Kosovo in October 1448 - the first battle happened in 1389 between Serbian prince Lazar Hrebeljanović and Sultan Murad I Hüdavendigâr.

With the Balkan front secured and the Ottoman directive firmly entrenched in the Danube, Murad II turned to Wallachia in 1449, forcing them to accept Ottoman authority in a bid to punish them for supporting John Hunyadi. He then turned east to do battle with Shah Rokh, Timur's son, and the emirates of Çorum-Amasya and Karamanid. In 1450, he led his forces to attack the resistance led by the military commander Gjergj Kastrioti (also known as Skanderbeg) in Albania, where he tried without success to take over the castle of Kruje.

Murad II fell ill in the winter of 1450-1451 and died in Edirne to be succeeded by his son Mehmed II who ruled from 1451-1481. The death of Murad II led the Ottomans to understand how unreliable and unsustainable a dynasty founded on the vassal system could be. They also realized that creating and maintaining a united empire left no other option but to establish direct Ottoman supremacy.

# Chapter Three:

## The Reign of the Conqueror

M ehmed II ascended the throne for the second time at the age of 21 in 1451. After his ascension, he erected a massive fortress called Rumelihisarı or Boğazkesen Castle (1452) between the Bosphorus straits (northwest Turkey, forming part of the continental boundary between Europe and Asia.) This fortress divided Turkey by separating Anatolia from Greece. Together with the Anadoluhisarı historically known as Güzelce "Hisar" or "the beautiful castle" on the Anatolian or Asian side of the Bosphorus, he gained total control of the channel.

Mehmed went a step further by imposing a levy on ships passing within reach of their cannons situated along these channels. Once, a Venetian ship blatantly ignored signals to stop and was blasted and sunk with a single shot. All surviving crewmen were beheaded with the captain impaled and hung as a human scarecrow to deter other sailors from plying the channel. With a strong navy, he laid a 53-day long siege on Constantinople from April 6 1453 till May 29 1453.

The Ottoman forces in this siege consisted of artillery of over 70 large field pieces, 80,000- 200,000 soldiers, and 320 naval ships, with the majority of them being transport and storage vessels. The Ottomans surrounded Constantinople on land and sea, with their maritime fleet stretching end to end, from the beginning of the Bosphorus straits in the form of a crescent cutting off any assistance for Constantinople.

The siege ultimately brought an end to the Byzantine rule. Many Muslim scholars regarded this battle as a fulfillment of a divine prophecy of the Musnad (hadith) by Ahmad ibn Hanbal and a sign of the impending apocalypse. This victory earned Mehmed II the title of Caesar Quyser-i Rûm of the Roman Empire, based on the fact that the city of Constantinople had been the seat of the eastern Roman dynasty following its consecration in 330 AD by emperor Constantine I.

Mehmed II erected the Eyüp Sultan Mosque with Ottoman architect Mimar Sinan at the tomb of Abu Ayyub al-Ansari, a patron of early Muslim history who supported the prophet Muhammad (SAW) in the migration or hijra to Medina. Abu Ayyub al-Ansari died of dysentery during the first siege of Constantinople (674-678). The mosque Mehmed erected on his gravesite was to display the importance of this conquest to Islamic history and solidify his role as ghâzi.

After the siege, the Sultan passed through the Topkapi gate (now a large museum in the east of Fatih district of Istanbul, Turkey). He rode his horse to the Hagia Sofia, which was built in 537 as a Christian cathedral. He ordered the building to be heavily guarded and sent for an imam to meet him. The Muslim creed "Ash-hadu anla elaha illa-Al-lah wa ash-hadu anna Mhammadur rasul-Allah," meaning, "There is no other God but Allah and Muhammad is his messenger" was chanted. There and then, the Sultan, with the help of the Ottoman architect Sinan-i Atik transformed the largest ca-thedral of the eastern Roman Empire to the grand faith mosque, which further cemented Islamic re-ligion in the city of Constantinople. Mehmed II also captured the Trapezuntine Empire in northern

Anatolia in 1461. Historians claim that ten years after seizing Constantinople, Mehmed II visited Troy to boast of his victory, stating that he had conquered the Byzantines and avenged the Trojans.

The conquest of eastern Christianity made room for the Ottomans to gain more control over sea trade routes from the Black Sea to the Mediterranean, one of the most strategic and vital international trade lines. In 1456, three years after seizing Constantinople, the Ottomans conquered Belgrade, threatening Hungary. Hunyadi launched a counterattack in Serbia while Vlad III Dracula led his troops into Wallachia to take back his motherland and slaughter the impostor Vladislaus II.

Mehmed's power-hungry crusade to force Ottoman rule over the entire Balkan region started with the seizure of the Morea in 1458. This was the territory of the southern Ottoman Balkans known as the Peloponnese peninsula or Peloponnesus, located in the south of Greece.

In 1459, Mehmed sent messengers to Vlad III. The aim was to compel him to pay a delayed tribute in the form of a tariff as proof of allegiance and respect. The tax was in the way of 10,000 ducats and 500 men recruited into the Ottoman military. Vlad III refused and killed the Sultan's messengers by nailing their turbans to their heads, using the excuse that the messengers refused to take off their "hats" in respect by saying they only removed their headgear before the almighty Allah.

In response to this insult, the Sultan sent Hamza Paşa, the admiral (Bey) of Nicopolis, to barter peace and, if needed, eliminate Vlad III. Vlad was prepared for this and laid an ambush. He caught and impaled many Ottomans. The Bey was impaled on the highest stake as was befitting for his rank. In the winter of 1462, Vlad crossed the Danube river. He set fire to Bulgarian territory between the black sea and Serbia. Vlad III then disguised himself as a Turkish Sipahi (cavalryman), and using his superior command of the Turkish language and customs, invaded Ottoman camps, killing and capturing several Ottoman armies. He then wrote a letter to Corvinus mentioning how he massacred peasants, both male and female, young and old. These peasants lived at Oblucitza and Novoselo, at points where the Danube flowed into the sea up to Rahova in southwest Bucharest Romania, west of the Dâmbovița river located near Chilia. He also mentioned killing 23,884 Turks, excluding those burnt alive in their homes and those beheaded by his soldiers.

At the time raiding Corinth, the Ottoman sultan decided to launch a savage attack to discipline Vlad the Impaler in Wallachia. Because Vlad was dead set on killing the Sultan, Mehmed suffered many casualties while trying to attack Vlad in a surprise night raid. When Mehmed II and Radu the handsome (younger brother to Vlad the Impaler and prince of the principality of Wallachia) arrived at Târgoviște (the seat of the Dâmbovița county), they saw so many Ottomans impaled. Shocked by the mere sight, the Sultan considered turning tail but was convinced by his army generals to stand his ground.

Vlad's idea of eternal resistance against the Ottomans was a hard pill for some to swallow. Vlad's stubbornness led to a betrayal by local aristocrats — the boyars, most of whom were pro-Dănești (rivals to the kingdom). Vlad was also let down by Stephen III of Moldavia, who promised help in defeating the Turks but turned around to attack Vlad in a bid to claim the fortress of Chilia for himself. Shaken by this betrayal, Vlad escaped to the mountains allowing the Ottomans with the help of the Ottoman general Turahanoğlu Ömer Bey, son of the famed Turahan Bey, to gain control of the Wallachian capital. Ömer Bey singlehandedly wiped out 6,000 Wallachians, throwing the head of at least 2,000 at his Sultan's feet.

Mehmed withdrew his forces, but not before enthroning his ally Radu as the king of Wallachia. Ömer Bey, in reward for his services, got reinstated in the old Thessaly gubernatorial position. Vlad ran from his hideout in the mountains to Hungary. There, accused of heresy against his sovereign Mattias Corvinus, who was the Hungarian and Croatian king, son of John Hunyadi, regent of Hungary, Vlad was imprisoned. Historians claim that while Vlad was in prison, he caught small birds and rats and impaled them on tiny sticks. In 1476, Vlad was ambushed by Ottoman soldiers and decapitated. His head was sent as a prize to the Sultan in Constantinople.

Mehmed also faced resistance in Albania against Gjergj Kastrioti, widely known as Skanderbeg.

Skanderbeg kept fighting the Ottomans while repeatedly asking the Italians for help. He fought Ottomans from 1443 till his demise in 1468. After his death, the Albanians were without a leader, which allowed Mehmed II to conquer Albania and Kruje in 1478. This battle known in history, known as the fourth siege of Shkodra was a siege personally led by Mehmed. Ottoman history buff Franz Babinger described it as one of the most iconic events in the power struggle between the west and the crescent. Far east, the Ottomans emerged victorious in their fight against the Aq Qoyunlu confederation and their ruler Uzun Hasan, the ninth Shahanshah who presided over the southern Caucasus and the city of Iran in the battle of Otlukbeli which took place in the summer of 1473.

Sultan Mehmed II is famous for instituting the word "politics" into Arabic literature, also known as Siyāsah. He also published a collection of the political doctrines of the Byzantine Caesars preceding him. He allowed the Byzantine church to continue operations but ordered the patriarch Gennadius II, a Byzantine theologian, and philosopher, to translate Christian teachings to Turkish. As an avid art collector, he commissioned portraits and Venetian frescoes (now missing) to be painted by Gentile Bellini, an Italian painter from Venice. He founded a university, built waterways for trade and transport, as well as other edifices such as the tiled kiosk (a pavilion within the outer Topkapi palace), the Topkapi palace itself, and the eight madrasas called Sahn-ı Seman Medrese, or Semâniyye, or the eight courtyards.

The madrasas were part of the faith mosque, serving as the highest educational facilities for the sciences like mathematics, medicine, law, theology, astrology, physics, etc. The building stood for over a century as a pillar of education in the Islamic Empire. Later on, in Constantinople, Mehmed II set up a millet, appointing Gennadius Scholarius as the Christian faction's religious leader.

This power extended to all Ottoman and Turkish Orthodox Christians, excluding the Venetian and Genoese settlements and the Jewish and Muslim practitioners. This way, the Sultan had authority over the Christians even after the Turkish remodeling and repopulation of Constantinople. One major milestone Mehmed II was able to accomplish was the Ḳānūnnāme, which was a legal code, generally known as the decree of the Sultan.

The code went against tradition and the decrees of his predecessors and served as a welcome change in a stagnated empire unwilling to change due to deep traditional roots. With the new order, he delegated more power and responsibilities to the vezirs than the other sultans. He also erected walls around the palace, making him inaccessible to lower-ranked officials and the public. The vezirs were in charge of enlisting the military and meeting with foreign ambassadors, one of which was kinsman Karaböcü Kuzen Paşa, who hailed from a family of spies and played a vital role in Mehmed's victory in Constantinople.

In 1481, Mehmed, while marching with his army, fell ill in Maltepe, Istanbul. He had set up plans to seize south Italy and Rhodes and conquer the Mamluk sultanate in Egypt to take the caliphate. Sultan Mehmed II died on May 3, 1481, at the age of 49.

There is strong evidence that he was poisoned at the instruction of his eldest son Bayezid II, also called Bayezid the saint. Mehmed II was buried in a tomb ("Türbe" in Turkish) beside the Fatih mosque. His death caused an uproar in Europe among the Christians who rang church bells and threw festivals in glee. Word spread throughout Venice, thus, "La Grande Aquila è morta!" which translated means "The great eagle is dead."

Mehmed II is one of the three greatest Ottoman sultans (the two others are Süleyman I and Selim I). Mehmed II was the first ruler to structure constitutional and criminal law, establishing the traditional image of the autocratic Ottoman ruler. Feared by many and regarded as a bloodthirsty tyrant by critics, he is a national hero in Turkey. The Fatih Sultan Mehmet bridge completed in 1988 was named after him, with his image and name engraved on the 1,000 lira note from 1986-1992.

# Chapter Four:

## The Saint in the Shadows

Bāyezīd-i ṣānī or Bayezid II the just born on December 3 1447 to Mehmed II and Gülbahar Hatun (also known as Mükrime Hatun). When Sultan Mehmed II died, Bayezid, the eldest, was in his early thirties. By his right as the eldest son, he was to inherit the throne. However, Mehmed II's new decree made things a little tricky.

According to the new decree, any son could ascend the throne. Fratricide was an acceptable means to do so as long as it happened for the people's common good. This law didn't give a line for succession; it only reiterated that every prince was on his own, and only the strongest or luckiest would rule after his death. After Mehmed's demise, envoys loyal to the different princes rode out to alert them to the situation.

The grand vizier Karamanlı Mehmed Paşa decided to break Islamic law to have the deceased

Sultan's remains brought to Constantinople where it lay in state for three days. He did this to give Çem, (pronounced jem) Mehmed's favorite, enough time to get to the capital. Bayezid II may have been the eldest, but Çem had a dubious argument in his favor. Çem claimed he was next in line for the throne since he was the first son of Mehmed to be "Porphyrogenitus," meaning born in the purple. Porphyrogenitus was a royal title bestowed on princes born in the purple room of Constantinople's royal palace. Çem argued that his "imperial porphyry" made him the rightful successor to the Ottoman throne over Bayezid II. It is worth mentioning that the so-called purple room was not available to the Ottomans before 1453, the year Constantinople fell, six years after the birth of Bayezid.

While Çem was grasping at straws in his bid to rule, the Janissaries backed Bayezid II and informed him of the grand vizier's delay tactics. Following orders from Bayezid, the Janissaries responded the only way they knew how. They hung the vizier and created a ruckus in an otherwise peaceful empire. With the constant riots, political killings, and princes racing on horseback to the capital, people were scared for their lives.

Çem's strategy consisted of capturing towns around Bursa to strengthen political ties, while Bayezid, on the other hand, was the first to arrive at the capital. He donned the belt, sword, and armor of Osman I to legitimize his claim to the throne. Çem's strategy looked fickle compared to Bayezid's, and showed his lack of experience.

Bayezid then seized the opportunity to raise an army, sending his newly appointed vizier Ayas Mehmed Paşa to crush Çem and his rebellion in the Bursa. Çem beat the inexperienced vizier in battle and took to minting coins in his name proclaiming himself Sultan. At some point, he offered his brother Bayezid an option to split the Ottoman Empire 50-50, where he would have Europe and Çem himself rule over Anatolia.

Bayezid's response was more exciting than a swift refusal. He raised a new army and, to ensure victory, led the troops himself. He defeated Çem, who escaped from the battlefield and boarded a ship headed to Egypt's Mamluk sultanate. The Mameluk sultanate welcomed the prince warmly. Çem saw Egypt not just as a hideout but as a place where he could strategize a takeover in safety and conveniently plan for the Hajj in Mecca. This escape is why Çem was the only Sultan to complete the holy pilgrimage.

Çem kept escaping his brother's clutches until he landed in Knights Hospitaller of St. John on the island of Rhodes. This is somewhat ironic given that the Rhodes are the ideological enemies of the Ottoman empire. During his exile in Rhodes, Çem was treated not as a prisoner, but as a blue-blooded guest under house arrest. Each time Bayezid wanted to invade the west, his brother's life dangled like a bargaining chip. At the urging of Pope Innocent VIII, the Sultan agreed to a hefty annual tribute of 45,000 ducats for his brother's expenses.

As the supreme ruler of the empire, Bayezid's main concern apart from his troublesome brother was the Ottoman dynasty's consolidation. Bayezid adopted a different approach from his father to rule the empire. Where Mehmed II would declare war, Bayezid II would broker peace. He strived to obtain consent and focus on dialogue instead of using brute force. Bayezid was not one to cringe at the sight of blood. People knew the Sultan knew that there were firm lines one could not cross. He wasn't opposed to the use of arms; he just preferred a balance of policies.

One of the occurrences that buttress this point was Bayezid's reaction to an open and surprisingly forward letter written by the Crimean Khan — descendants of Genghis khan — who became an Ottoman vassal in the 15th century. In the letter, the Khans blatantly asked the Sultan if the Jihad was no longer in force as the Ottoman army had been inactive for a considerably long time.

The Sultan replied in his usual calm but firm manner, stating that he was mindful of the importance of the Jihad and the blessings that accrue in both worlds, but that rulers had a primary responsibility before Allah to maintain peace in the land and ensure the prosperity of their subjects. He also added that order was an impossible feat when the Sultan and his troops were always in a state of conquest.

The differences in temperament between Bayezid and his father were so much that it seemed Bayezid lived primarily in his father's shadow. Like his father, he was also intrigued by mathematics, law, medicine, history, and literature. He also participated in sports such as archery and horseback riding and, unlike other sultans, was an established calligrapher. To cap it off, he was a pious Muslim who did not take kindly to a lot of his father's excesses, such as commissioning portraits and patronizing western artists to come to Istanbul. He sold off a considerable portion of Mehmed's collection and disposed of his statues. His dedication to Sharia law and the smooth day to day running of domestic politics earned him the title of Adil, meaning "the just," and Velî, meaning "the Saint."

Bayezid II, as underrated as most thought he was, had several notable conquests in his reign as a sultan. He embarked on a mission to extend the Ottoman empire to the northern and western shores of the Black Sea. He did this by going to war with Moldavia and seizing Akkerman and Kilia's fortresses on the Black Sea in 1484, Cătlăbuga in 1485, and Scheia in 1486. These invasions brought the Poles into conflict with the Ottomans.

The second Ottoman-Venetian war took place under Sultan Bayezid II for control of the lands bordering the Aegean Sea, as well as the Adriatic and the Ionian Sea. The Ottomans emerged victorious in the conquest of Lepanto and Mothoni on the Mediterranean in 1499-1500, as well as the Durrës (Durazzo) on the Adriatic in 1501.

Bayezid II took steps to improve the naval forces of the Ottoman state. While this was not as grandiose a conquest as capturing Constantinople, he was responsible for commanding Admiral Kemal Reis to send the Ottoman naval fleet to Spain in 1492. The navy's singular mission was to evacuate the Muslim and Jewish populations who were forcefully evicted from the new state of Spain during the "Tribunal of the Holy Office of the Inquisition," also called the Spanish Inquisition. The examination was established in 1478 by Ferdinand II of Aragon and Isabella I of Castille, both Catholic monarchs in their own right. The aim behind the inquisition was to maintain Orthodox Catholic religion in their kingdoms.

The Sultan granted the fugitives leave to settle in his empire to take up Ottoman citizenship. The Sultan mocked the Catholic monarchs' action to his courtiers, saying that Ferdinand had impoverished his country to enrich the Ottoman state. The new refugees made significant contributions to the rising power of the Ottoman empire by bringing new ideas, craftsmanship, and methods to the fore. The Hispanic or Sephardi Jews founded the first printing press in Constantinople in 1493.

The Jews flourished during Bayezid's reign with scientists and scholars such as Mordecai Comtino, poets like Shabbethai ben Malkiel Cohen, and astronomer Solomon ben Elijah Sharbiṭ ha-Zahab. Bayezid II was responsible for the continued economic development of Bursa and Edirne. He built two complexes and mosques, one just outside Edirne and notable for its advanced healthcare services, and the other on the third hill of Constantinople (modern-day Istanbul University and the Grand Bazaar). He also commissioned the Galatasaray (palace of Galata) to be built as a place of learning for young boys who would grow up to one day serve the empire.

Bayezid was known to be tolerant of other religions. This tolerance led him to exempt the lands on mount Athos (modern-day Greece) belonging to the Koutloumousiou Monastery from paying tithes. The local Muslims kept tormenting the monks and peasants who farmed the grounds for these monks, forcing them to pay taxes. Bayezid got wind of this and ordered the Subaci (governor) and the Kadi (judges of Islamic law) in Thessaloniki to enforce an imperial edict granting the monks tithe exemptions and the restoration of any seized properties.

At this time, a far more powerful force was brewing in the east. The rise of the Shia Safavid dynasty caused the Ottomans to direct their energies toward eastern Anatolia, where the power and growing popularity of the Iranian ruler, Shah Ismail, posed a danger to the Ottoman rule. Ismail's Safavid forces conquered Baghdad in 1504 and permeated southwestern Anatolia.

There were a series of destructive earthquakes plaguing northern Anatolia, Istanbul, and Edirne. Bayezid II had advanced in years and became ill. He had lost whatever influence he had on the Janissaries who had backed up his son Selim. As a result, Bayezid was unable to organize his forces to obliterate the Safavids. Emboldened by his support from the Janissaries, Selim forced his father to abdicate the throne in his favor. Bayezid left for early retirement in Demotika, but died a month after his abdication on May 26 1512. The Sultan passed away at Havsa, near Büyükçekmece, in the suburbs of Istanbul. He never got to his destination. Sources claim that the Sultan died by a Jewish physician's poison as he was about to go into exile. These sources claim that the new Sultan Selim had a motive. Bayezid was buried next to Bayezid mosque in Constantinople beside one of his daughters, Ayşe Hatun.

# Chapter Five:

# The Zenith of the Empire and the Sword of the Grim

A s soon as Bayezid began to display weakness and signs of ill health, the issue of succession to the throne intensified. Sultan Bayezid II had five sons, two of whom had passed; thus, the contenders to the throne were the remaining three adult princes. The eldest and the most loved was Şehzade Ahmet, appointed by his father to govern Amasya. The second prince, Şehzade Korkut, was educated at his grandfather Mehmed II's court in music, Islamic law, sciences, and poetry. He was the governor of Antalya. The last prince, the astute and crafty Selim, was governor of Trabizon in the Black Sea region of Anatolia.

Selim had garnered the support of the Janissaries when the issue of the Safavid Iranians was at its peak. Young prince Selim was born on October 10 1470 to his majesty Sultan Şehzade Bayezid (later

Bayezid II), and Gülbahar Hatun in Amasya. Selim was infuriated by his father's announcement proclaiming Ahmet as the next in line. He rebelled against his father in the Ottoman civil war, a battle of succession between the two brothers Selim and Ahmet from 1509-1512. Selim emerged the victor and forced his father to abdicate to him before sending him on exile to Demotika.

Sultan Selim ascended the throne to overrule his father's peacemaking approach to neighboring nations. He wished to reinstate the aggressive and brutal policies of his grandfather Mehmed II, which in his eyes served a larger purpose: The expansion of the empire. The primary instrument Selim used to drive his point across was the Janissaries, whose powers had tripled during his reign. Not wanting any form of anarchy regarding the line of succession to the Ottoman throne, Selim swiftly executed his brothers Şehzade Ahmet and Şehzade Korkut, as well as all of his nephews. This action earned him the title of Yavuz, meaning grim, stern, or resolute.

Only one nephew of his, Şehzade Murad (son of Ahmet the legitimate heir), managed a narrow escape to the Safavid Empire after failing to amass enough support to stake his claim to the throne. Selim left only one male alive, his son Süleyman, to ensure a peaceful succession to the throne after his passing, the continuation of power, and the continued consolidation of the empire.

One of the matters arising following Selim's ascension was the issue of neutralizing the growing tension from Shah Ismāʿīl's forces. The Safavids were no small fry. Under their leader Ismāʿīl I, they had enjoyed high power and status in eastern Anatolia and among Turcoman tribes who had settled in northern Syria. Since converting to Shia Islam, Ismāʿīl and his men had taken to wearing unique headgear, one with twelve triangles which stood for the twelve Shia Islamic religious leaders known as Kizilbaş or Qizilbaş (redheads).

Shah Ismāʿīl had visions of transforming the Persian Empire, which stretched from the plains of central Asia to the shores of the Mediterranean. By the year 1511, Ismāʿīl had started a Safavid or pro-Shia revolt known as the Şahkulu Rebellion in Anatolia. Selim did not take this chaos lightly. He knew that invading eastern Anatolia could not be limited to merely defeating Ismāʿīl's army. The Sultan knew that apart from the redheads, he had a duty to uproot all urban and rural networks established by the Safavids and their troops. Thus, when the Ottoman army invaded central and eastern Anatolia, they slaughtered tens of thousands of supporters suspected of being Safavid sympathizers. The dead bodies were displayed publicly on the roads to deter anyone from joining forces with Ismāʿīl's and the Shia Muslims.

Selim and Ismāʿīl's then proceeded to exchange a series of hostile letters. Selim wrote three, and Ismāʿīl's wrote one in response. In the letters, Selim defended his right to rule by quoting Quranic verses, subtly calling his rival a usurper. Ismāʿīl's, on the other hand, based his claim based on inheritance. He insisted that he was a direct descendant of Ali, the son in law of Prophet Muhammad (SAW), and remained the only living legitimate successor in all lands. Ismāʿīl's addressed his rival Selim in a careless and somewhat discourteous tone, which made the Sultan and his army launch an attack on the Safavid troops in a battle that took place on the plains of Châldiran, northeast of Lake Van on August 23 1514.

The Shia Islamic (Safavid) forces were defeated by the Ottoman, who were armed to the teeth with muskets and artillery. The Safavid armies were forced to retreat while the Turks made their way to the heart of Azerbaijan. They occupied Tabriz, which served as the military, political, and administrative seat of Safavid authority. After the battle, Selim stated that his rival Ismā'īl's was always intoxicated to the point of no return and was completely negligent regarding matters of the state.

An early and harsh winter brought the Ottomans an unexpected attack from Safavid troops. The Safavid army seriously vexed the Turks, cutting off their water and food rations. This incident, together with increased pressure mounted on Sultan Selim by the janissaries to return, forced him to return with his troops to eastern Anatolia. As the two empires, the Safavid and the Ottomans failed to broker a treaty, attacks and confrontations continued for the next forty years. However, the Ottomans were the stronger of the two forces. Although the Ottoman army withdrew from Azerbaijan, their victorious conquest at Châldiran put an end to the looming threat by the Shia Safavids. Selim had free rein to enforce Ottoman rule over a large part of Kurdistan and eastern Anatolia.

Selim then decided to center his forces in Egypt and Syria, which had been governed by the Mamluk sultanate since the 13th century. The Ottomans saw the Mamluks as irritants for two significant reasons: They frequently provided a sanctuary for defiant and disgruntled Ottoman princes, and they also offered countless usurpers to the Ottoman throne. Also, the Mamluks had taken Cicilia in southern Anatolia for themselves, which prevented the Ottomans from approaching the Arabs. In addition to the reasons stated above, the Mamluks had also conquered Medina and Mecca, the most sacred places in Islamic history. These "advantages" possessed by the Mamluks were the principal reasons why the Ottomans felt a need to conquer them.

Sultan Selim and his troops garrisoned Dulkadir, which served as a barrier between the Mamluks and the Ottomans. The Sultan's army invaded Syria and wreaked havoc on the Mamluks in the battle of Marj Dabiq, north of Aleppo (modern-day Syria) on August 24 1516. In this battle, Selim killed the Mamluk sultan, Al-Ashraf Qansuh al-Ghawri. After that, the cities of Damascus, Jerusalem, and Aleppo bowed to the Ottoman rule.

After the capture of Damascus, Selim restored the tomb of the famous Arab Andalusian scholar, poet, philosopher, and Sufi (Islamic mysticism) master. His name was Abū 'Abd Allāh Muḥammad ibn 'Alī ibn Muḥammad ibn ʿArabī al-Ḥātimī aṭ-Ṭāʾī al-Andalusi al-Mursi al-Dimashqi, fondly called Ibn Arabi. Ibn Arabi was a highly revered Muslim scholar who died on November 8 1240.

Shortly after, Selim defeated the Mamluk forces once again, this time under the command of Al-Ashraf Tuman Bëy II in the battle of Ridanieh on January 22 1517. The Ottomans severed Tuman Bëy's head and hung it on a gate at the entrance to the Ghourieh quarter of Cairo. Hadim Sinan Paşa, Selim's grand vizier, was also killed in battle. The Turks conquered the entire Mamluk sultanate from Palestine in Sham, Syria, Hejaz, Tihamah in the Arabian Peninsula, and Egypt.

Al-Mutawakkil III, the 17th and last ruler of the Mamluk sultanate (also known as the final Abbasid caliph) was a mere figurehead residing in

Cairo during Selim's conquest of Egypt. Selim sent Al-Mutawakkil III into exile to Istanbul. Historians say that in the 18th century, the last Mamluk caliph transferred his title, sword, emblems, and the mantle of Muhammad to the Ottoman sultan. These artifacts are present in the Topkapi palace museum in Istanbul turkey. Claiming the Mamluk caliph is why Selim is known as the first Sultan to assume the title of Caliph of Islam in Ottoman history.

Selim's back to back victories earned him the title of Ḥākimü'l-Ḥaremeyn, or "the protector of The Two Holy Cities." Still, the Sultan rejected that title in favor of the more pious Ḥādimü'l-Ḥaremeyn, or "servant of the two holy cities."

Selim was well known for his fiery temperament and his habit of expecting a lot from his subordinates. A lot of his viziers were killed for various petty reasons. A popular Ottoman expletive goes, "May you be a vizier of Selim." This curse calls back to the sheer number of viziers the Sultan had massacred.

There is a famous story about a vizier who had jokingly asked the Sultan for prior notice of his anger so that he would have enough time to get his home in order. The Sultan laughed and told the vizier that killing him had been at the forefront of his mind, but he could not find a replacement for him as yet. He added that once he was able to, he would happily put him to death. On the advice of some influential Ottoman clerics and courtiers, Selim issued a proclamation that placed a death sentence on anyone who dared use the German printing press (invented in 1455) to print any Turkish or Arabic texts.

On the flip side, Selim was an accomplished poet with tons of Persian and Turkish poetry written under the pen name Mahlas Selimi. Copies of some of his works are still in circulation today, while many others are extinct. He was also good at archery, fencing, and wrestling, perhaps because of his penchant for fighting. Selim remained one of the greatest rulers of the Ottoman Empire, highly respected for his work ethic. During the brief period of his reign, the Ottoman Empire reigned supreme, spanning three continents with vast holdings in Asia, Europe, and Africa. With a population of over 15 million Ottomans, Selim's reign spelled the zenith of Ottoman sovereignty and prepared a smooth foundation for his heir and successor, Sü-leyman.

Legend has it that Selim filled the royal coffers to the brink with treasures and gold. He locked it with his seal and decreed that whoever surpassed him or filled the treasury to the level he did was free to secure it with their seal. No ruler ever achieved that feat, so the royal treasury was locked with Selim's seal and remained inaccessible until the decline and collapse of the Ottoman dynasty 400 years later.

Selim is famous for inventing the Taylesanlı Se-limi turban, a style of headgear with one end of the wrap hanging down. He wore this on top of an even more impressive headdress called the Mücevveze, a red velvet turban of sorts similar to the one worn by the Janissaries. The Sultan was a man of simple yet modern tastes. His simplicity was evident in his food and feeding utensils (he had one particular wooden plate and utensil), and manner. Even his attire was a simple cut and design similar to the one worn by the Gâzi.

Selim soon suffered age and disease. He was said to have Sirpence, an anthrax infection seen on the skin of leather artisans and livestock workers.

This infection was suspected because he lived half his life on horseback. Other accounts claim that he died of cancer and poisoning by the physician treating his skin infection. The majority of the sources, however, have evidence that Selim's demise coincided with a period of plague in Ottoman history.

The Sultan's eight-year reign came to a close on September 22 1520, when he passed at age 49, at Çorlu Tekirdağ. Upon his death, he was brought to Istanbul and buried in the Yavuz Selim mosque commissioned by his son Süleyman, in loving memory of his king and father.

# Chapter Six:

## The Reign of the Magnificent

U pon the death of Selim I, his son and heir Sü-leyman-ı Evvel, born on November 6, 1494, had been groomed by his father to take the reins. He ascended the throne at the age of 26 and lived from 1520 to 1566. The new Sultan was intent on conquering Hungary. This victory would allow the Ottomans to establish a connection to central Europe and mount intense pressure on the Habsburgs. This mission was aided by the French king Francis I (1515-1547), who had no love lost for Charles V (1519-1547), the Habsburg emperor.

The Ottomans capitalized on the rivalry and division among the European nations, which is why they were at the forefront championing Calvinism through Europe, especially in Hungary. Süleyman began his reign by planning a campaign against Belgrade, which controlled the road to the Hungarian south plains. The Ottoman forces attacked and conquered Belgrade on August 29, 1521. His victory in Belgrade fulfilled his great-grandfather Mehmed II's mission to rule Belgrade, which failed as a result of Hunyadi's vigorous defense of the region.

The same year, Süleyman suppressed an uprising led by the Ottoman-appointed governor of Damascus. The Sultan then turned his sights to Rhodes under the leadership of the Knight Hospitallers of Saint John, forcing them to withdraw after a prolonged battle on January 21, 1522. By 1525, the animosity between the two European monarchs Charles V and Francis I led to open warfare, which led to the French king's capture and imprisonment. The arrest prompted France to seek Ottoman assistance and provided a golden opportunity for the Ottomans needed to attack the Hungarian army. The Hungarians lacked the Turks' cohesion and unity and fell to their defeat in one of the most famous battles in history: The Battle of Mohács fought on August 29, 1526.

Charles V and his brother Ferdinand I, ruler of Austria's neighboring lands, led the Habsburgs to reoccupy Buda and take charge of Hungary. Süleyman responded to this insult in 1529 by marching with his troops through the Danube valley. The Sultan regained possession of Buda and the following year, planned an attack on Vienna, one that was said to be Süleyman's most outrageous mission yet, showing the extent to which he wanted to take charge of the west.

The Austrians in revenge for the incident at Buda attacked the Ottomans with a reinforced cavalry of 16,000 men. The attack led to the beginning of a bitter Habsburg-Ottoman feud, one that lasted till the end of the 20th century. Süleyman's 2nd attempt at overtaking Vienna failed in 1532 following the delay caused by the siege of Kőszeg. Here, the Ottomans suffered deplorable weather conditions that forced them to abandon essential weapons.

The Sultan then decided to establish Ottoman rule over the Mediterranean's shores, where Genoa and Venice had once held sway. He appointed the famous Hayreddin Paşa, also known as Barbarossa, the Kupdan-I Deryâ or grand admiral of the Ottoman troops, to proceed with the expansion of the Ottoman dynasty to the north of Africa. There, they seized Tunis in August 1533 and bullied the residents occupying the Venetian islands of the Io-nian Sea.

This act of terrorism was the Ottoman way of sending a warning to Genoa, Portugal, Venice, and Spain that their empires were nothing but a giant sea they would have to defend. The late summer of 1533 saw the invasion of Iran by the Ottomans. The death of Safavid leader Ismāʿīl had created a vacuum and significantly weakened the Iranian forces' strength. Ismāʿīl ten-year-old son Tahmasp had no love for his father's methods. This stemmed from the fact that he had been used as a pawn countless times. Especially during disagreements between the commanders and their rivals the redheads.

Tahmasp dispatched several envoys to European courts to seek an alliance of sorts with the Ottomans. The Ottoman forces ignored the memo and proceeded to attack Safavid territory in 1534, capturing Mesopotamia and Azerbaijan under the command of the grand vizier Pargali Ibrahim Paşa. Bitlis and Tabriz fell into Süleyman's hands once more in July of 1534. To surpass his father, the Sultan made his troops go farther east to Sultaniyya before heading west, crossing the Zagros mountains to arrive at Baghdad, which he captured after a brief battle in November.

The fall of Baghdad and the early invasion of Egypt solidified the Ottoman empire as the supreme power in the middle east, a prestige they enjoyed until 1918, after the end of the first world war. In 1537, the Ottoman navy ambushed Venetia. They blocked off Corfu and terrorized Italy. The rising supremacy of the Ottoman navy on the Mediterranean and the Aegean Sea left Venice no other choice but to beg for peace in October 1540.

The same year, the continued conflict in Hungary granted Süleyman another window to avenge his loss at Vienna. The Habsburgs attempted another siege on Vienna but were deterred. As a result, the Ottomans captured even more Habsburgs fortresses in two consecutive wars in 1541 and 1544. The European monarchs Ferdinand I and Charles V had to sign a mortifying 5-year long treaty with the Ottomans. Ferdinand relinquished his claim to the Hungarian throne and levied a fixed annual tariff to the Sultan for the Hungarian lands under Ottoman rule. The treaty's symbolic importance was the reference to Charles V, not as an emperor, but as the Spanish king and Süleyman as the real Caesar.

Regardless of the hardships the Ottomans faced in battling Iran, Süleyman once more tried to capture Safavid territory in 1548 after Shah Tahmasp's brother Elqas Mirza fled to Ottoman lands seeking protection and assistance from the Sultan. Süleyman was sure that this internal strife over the Iranian throne could benefit the expansion of the Ottoman empire. He hatched a plan in which he teamed up with Elqas, sending an army with him to Safavid lands. This plan failed to establish the Ottoman rule in Iran.

The new alliance between the Iranian pretender Elqas Mirza and Süleyman soon went south after a disagreement that Elqas had with his new allies, the Ottomans. After this incident, Süleyman withdrew his support for the Iranian usurper. In 1553, Süleyman lost lands in Erzurum to Shah Tahmasp. He retaliated by conquering Erzurum, crossing the upper Euphrates, and destroying parts of Persia. The shah continued to avoid confrontation with the Ottomans, leading to a standoff between the two forces: The Turks and the Safavids.

On May 29 1555, in a bid to avoid costly military campaigns, the two parties signed the Amasya peace treaty. This treaty led to the equal division of Armenia and Georgia. Regions of western Georgia and Samtskhe, west Armenia, and western Kurdistan stayed with the Safavids. The majority of Iraq, including Baghdad, which granted access to the Gulf of Persia, Tabriz, and other northwestern lands in the Caucasus such as Dagestan and Azerbaijan, belonged to the Ottomans.

In 1559 after the first Ajran-Portuguese war, the Ottomans claimed the feeble Adal sultanate, which allowed Ottoman expansion into Somalia and Africa's horns that lay on the south side of the red sea. The horn extended hundreds of kilometers into the Somali sea, the Gulf of Aden, and the Guardafui channels. This conquest further increased Ottoman influence in the Indian ocean and led to them becoming strong contenders for power with their allies, the Ajran empire of Portugal.

In 1564, Süleyman received a message from Aceh (modern-day Indonesia) from their Sultan Alauddin Riayat Syah al- Kahhar (1539-1571) requesting assistance in his fight against the

Portuguese. Thus began the Ottoman expedition of Aceh in 1565. This expedition was to give the Aceh sultanate some back up in their battle in Malacca against the Portuguese Empire.

Süleyman was known as Muhteşem ("the magnificent") in the West and Kanuni ("the lawgiver") by his Ottoman subjects. His title as Kanuni was due to his many reforms of the Ottoman legal system.

The supreme law of the empire was the Islamic sacred law or Shari'ah, which was beyond the Sultan. However, the kanun (a distinct form of canonical law) was entirely within the Sultan's control. The kanun covered matters about taxation, criminal law, and land ownership. Süleyman reviewed all the judgments and proclamations made by his predecessors to eliminate contradictions and repetitions. With the help of the grand mufti (an Islamic jurisconsult) named Ebussuud Efendi, a single legal statute was issued within the confines of Islamic law.

This new law — the kanun-I Osmani — was formulated to adapt to a rapidly expanding empire. The new Osman laws lasted for about 300 years.

Süleyman also played a significant role in protecting the Jews under his control. Urged by his favorite doctor, a Spanish Jew named Moses Hamon, he issued a royal decree (firman) denouncing the accusations of blood libels against the Jews. Before the firman, the Jews were accused of killing about 150 Christian children and reportedly using their blood in the baking of Matzos (a flatbread eaten by Jews in Passover), among other religious rituals.

The Jews at the time were also accused of poisoning wells and desecrating bread used by Christians during mass. Süleyman was famous for building complexes for higher education (graduates became imams), aqueducts, public baths, soup kitchens, libraries, hospitals, and low-cost residencies for his subjects. Notable works include the Süleymaniye mosque complex in Istanbul and the Selimiye Mosque in Edirne Merkez, Turkey. These two buildings to date remain fascinating pieces of Ottoman architecture in Turkey.

The Sultan was also responsible for building a complex in Aleppo (Damascus), rebuilding the walls of Jerusalem, and renovating the al-Kaʿbah al-Musharrafah (fondly called the Kaaba), a cubic building at the center of the Masjid al-Haram in Mecca, Saudi Arabia. The Kaaba serves as the most sacred architecture in Islam.

Under Süleyman's reign, the Ottoman Empire attained its height of art and cultural development. Imperial artistic clubs called Ehl-i Hiref or "community of the artisans" were established at the Topkapi Palace. These clubs attracted the most established artisans and craftsmen to the Sultan's court. The artisans were a mix of artists, calligraphers, bookbinders, goldsmiths, and jewelers from both the Islamic nations and the recently conquered European territories. This blend of Turkish, Arab, and European cultures made its unique mark in Ottoman history.

Süleyman was a generous patron of poetry. An accomplished poet himself, he wrote Turkish and Persian verse under the pen name Muhibbi, meaning "lover." Many of his poems have become famous Turkish proverbs. One popular verse he wrote goes, "Everyone aims at the same meaning, but many are the versions to the story." When his son Mehmed died of smallpox in 1543, he wrote a touching chronogram, an inscription with the words, "Peerless among princes, my Sultan Mehmed," to commemorate the year of his son's passing. Two of the most exceptional talents of the time, Fuzuli and Mahmud Abdülbâki, composed "Kasidas" — poetry in praise of the Sultan. In return, the Sultan showered them gifts and praise, honoring Abdülbâki with the title of Sultan ul- şuarâ, meaning "king of poets."

Süleyman defied the Ottoman tradition by marrying a woman from his harem. Her name was Hürrem Sultan. She was initially an Orthodox Christian from Ruthenian origins who later converted to Islam. Hürrem was famous for her red hair, which earned her the nickname "Roxelana."

Hürrem had considerable influence over her sultan husband. Her son Selim II was chosen to ascend the throne over his elder brother Şehzade Mustafa, son of Süleyman's first wife, Mahidevran Hatun. Mustafa's relationship with his father was uneasy at best. Despite reservations and warnings from the Janissaries, Süleyman ordered the execution of his son Mustafa. Mahmut Ağa, the right-hand man of Rüstem Paşa (an Ottoman statesman, grand vizier of Sultan Süleyman and husband to Süleyman's daughter Mihrimah Hatun) strangled

Mustafa, as Süleyman watched from behind the curtain.

People blamed Hürrem, Rüstem, and the Sultan for the unfair execution of prince Mustafa. Mustafa's death caused an uproar in Amasya, Konya, and Manisa. He was well respected and expected to assume the throne after his father on account of his courage and generosity. For his son-in-law's safety, Rüstem was dismissed from his position as grand vizier and sent off to exile in Istanbul. The poet Taşlicali Yâhya composed a beautiful eulogy for the dead Mustafa, similar to the one done for prince Çem.

Earlier, Süleyman executed his other son Bayezid (his son with Hürrem) and his four sons in 1561 on account of a rebellion. After 46 years of a prosperous rule, Süleyman died of natural causes at the age of 71 in 1566. Süleyman, to date, remains the longest-ruling Sultan of the Ottoman Empire, which at the time of his reign had a population of more than 25 million people. He was buried on November 28 1566 at the Süleymaniye Mosque in Istanbul, Turkey.

# Chapter Seven:

## The Dissolution

Ottoman historians generally believe that the empire became diluted with the reign of Selīm-i s̠ānī or Selim the Blond. Sultan Selim II succeeded Süleyman in September 1566. The new Sultan was fond of wine and women. For this reason, he was nicknamed Şarhos Selim or Selim, the Drunkard. Selim spent a lot of his time in the Dar üs- Saade (Felicity house) in the inner part of the Topkapi Palace. He left most of the palace duties to Sokollu Mehmed Paşa, his grand vizier who had served Süleyman and was presently married to Selim II's daughter Ismihan Sultan.

As Selim became more detached from Ottoman affairs, the influence of his grand vizier grew. Selim's wife Nur Banu Sultan (originally named Rachael and was of Jewish origin), mother of the future heir Murad III also participated in ruling the kingdom. For the first time in Ottoman history, the empire was in the clutches of a woman.

In 1568, the Ottomans invaded Yemen, coloniz-
ing Aden and Sana'a in 1569, establishing their authority over commerce and trade routes of the Red
Sea. In the northern frontier, a plan was hatched
in Constantinople to unite the Don and Volga by a
canal. This plan was to prevent Russian expansion
towards Ottoman northern borders.

In the summer of 1569, a large force of Janissaries embarked on a violent conquest to seize Astra-
khan's strategic town on the Caspian Sea and ter-
rorize the Iranian cities of Azerbaijan and south of
Caucasus. The Ottomans also wished to establish a
link with the Uzbeks, who were allies of the Ottomans in Central Asia. Despite Sokollu's best efforts,
this plan didn't take shape. The Ottoman army had
to rely on another partner — the Crimean Tatars
— to act as a shield against the Russian military on
the northern coast of the Black Sea. A more suc-
cessful raid was the Ottoman capture of the island
of Cyprus. This island served as a refuge for pirates
raiding Ottoman ships in the Mediterranean. By
September 1570 and 1571, the Ottomans captured
Nicosia and Famagusta, respectively.

The fall of Cyprus persuaded the Christians to unify their forces. This alliance led to the battle of Lepanto in October 1571. This victory at Lepanto was praised throughout Europe as the beginning of the end of the Ottoman rule. The empire's ships were restored within months only for the Ottomans to prove their might again by regaining control of the east of the Mediterranean in 1573. In 1574, the power of Tunis, which Spain had seized in 1572, returned to the Ottomans.

During his reign, Selim restored the status and wealth of his stepmother, Mahidevran Sultan, and constructed a tomb for his late brother, Prince Mustafa, who was strangled in 1553. Selim II died at the age of 50 on December 15, 1574, at the Topkapi Palace. He was buried at the Hagia Sofia grand mosque, Istanbul. With Selim's death, his eldest Murad III (1574-1595) ascended the throne and immediately executed all his five brothers. During his 21-year long reign, he was famous for his insatiable sexual appetite. This behavior was evident in the sheer number of concubines in his harem, his 102 named sons, and his countless number of daughters. The presence of so many women gave rise to intense rivalries, strife, jealousy, and drama.

The factions from these rivalries, together with Sokollu's Paşa's influence in court, always undermined the Sultan's abilities. Sokollu renewed peace treaties with Venice in 1575, and two years later, with the Polish and the Habsburg monarchy. In North Africa, the Ottomans exploited the internal strife in Morocco to conquer the country in 1578. Even with his superior abilities as a diplomat, Sokollu was unable to silence the factions in the harem. He was assassinated on October 11, 1579. His death ended his 15-year-long service to the Ottoman Empire as a legal representative and chief administrator of state affairs.

In 1577, Murad III declared war on the Safavids (1578-1580) against the terms of the Amasya peace treaty. The Sultan sought control over the Iranian monarchy following the death of Shah Tahmasp. Murad also tried to colonize America but dumped the idea after the Spanish navy attacked Ottoman ships. Murad's reign was the period of a financial meltdown in the empire. Training soldiers to keep up with advanced military tactics put considerable strain on the treasury. There was also a high level of inflation. This inflation, coupled with the population increase in Anatolia, led to bribery and corruption in the offices. During this period, wages were cut in half, food prices skyrocketed, and riots were rising.

Murad, in all this chaos, led a sedentary life. He never left the Topkapi palace for fear that the Janissaries would dethrone or execute him. When his mother Nurbanu died, he ensured she was laid to rest next to her husband, Selim II. This occurrence was the first time in history a consort was buried in a sultan's tomb. Murad III himself died of natural causes at 48 in the Topkapi Palace. He was buried in the Hagia Sofia mosque in Istanbul. His death brought about the reign of his son Mehmed III (1595-1603). With Mehmed's ascension, the new Sultan ordered the assassination of his 19 brothers and 20 sisters. Mehmed was a lazy ruler. He left matters of the state to his mother, Safiye Sultan, an Albanian from Dukagjin.

Mehmed III's major accomplishment was the Austro-Ottoman war in Hungary. This war started from an indecisive land dispute between the

Ottomans and the Habsburgs and lasted 13 years, from 1593 to 1606. Under the personal command of the Sultan, the Ottomans invaded Wallachia and captured Bucharest and Egar in 1596. Later in the battle of Kereztes (also known as the battle of Haçova) that lasted from 24th-26th October 1596, the Ottomans conquered Transylvania and the Habsburgs.

This victory was soon cut short by the significant losses that plagued the empire soon after, among them being the loss of Gyor to Austria and the defeat of Ottoman armies by Wallachians under the leadership of Michael the brave in 1599. Mehmed III died at 37 on December 22, 1603, from a sudden stroke. Other sources say he died from grief following the death of his son Mahmud. Some other sources claim he died from poisoning administered by his guard Dervish Mehmed Paşa. The Sultan was buried at the Hagia Sophia, and his 13-year-old son Ahmed I became the new Sultan. One notable event in Ahmed's reign was the abolition of fratricide.

Ahmed was also responsible for building the Sultan Ahmed Mosque (the Blue Mosque), the piece de resistance of Ottoman architecture just across the Hagia Sophia. The Sultan renovated the Kaaba, which had been ravaged by flood. In Ahmed's reign as Sultan, there were numerous losses. The most important of these were losing the annual tribute paid to the Ottoman empire by the Austrians following the treaty of Zsitvatorok, signed in 1606, and the defeat of the Ottomans in the Safavid war (1603-1618).

Sultan Ahmed died of typhus fever and gastric bleeding on November 22, 1617, at the Topkapi palace in Istanbul. He was laid to rest in a crypt just beside the Blue Mosque.

# Chapter Eight:

# The Decline and the Fall

I t is noteworthy to state that the Ottoman Empire didn't decline overnight. Historians claim that depreciation was already afoot during the reign of Süleyman, only manifesting itself centuries later. The defeat of the Ottoman forces by the Safavids during Ahmed's reign sabotaged Ottoman rule in the Arab world and Anatolia. Turkoman and Kurdish tribal chiefs fled, leading to riots in Syria where the Kurds staged a revolt against the Ottoman Empire.

When Sultan Ibrahim (1640-1648) ascended the throne, he was unfit to rule for two significant reasons: His high sexual appetite, and lack of experience. His assassination in Istanbul on the orders of Grand Vizier Mevlevî Mehmed Paşa led to the ascension of his son Sultan Mehmed IV (1648-1687).

In 1656, the Ottoman Empire was cracking under the strain of political and financial crises. Financial issues faced by an empty treasury, coupled with the Ottoman navy's inability to stop the Venetians who had seized their capital, led to the appointment of Köprülü viziers. The Köprülü family were statesmen from the noble Köprülü family of Albania, tasked to help in governing the empire. The new viziers introduced urgent reforms that turned things in the realm around.

On September 12 1683, the Habsburg monarch joined forces with Jan Sobieski of Poland, Spain, the Pope, and Portugal. This alliance led to Vienna's battle on the Kahlenberg mountains, where 10,000 Ottoman soldiers were murdered on the battlefield. This defeat caused the disintegration of the empire and the unity and cohesion the Ottoman army was known for.

In January 1699, the Ottomans signed the Karlowitz peace treaty with representatives of the Holy League Powers (Venice, Austria, Poland, and Russia). This treaty put to death whatever was left of the glory, prestige, and control of the Ottoman sultans past. By 1700, absolute Ottoman power had become nothing but a vague memory.

Extended battles with Venice, Russia, Poland, and the Habsburg monarchy had greatly depleted state resources. At this point, the empire could not even afford to pay the salaries of the soldiers and officials. Increases in financial corruption and partisanship forced Mustafa II (the Sultan at the time) to ask the Köprülü family's assistance once again for help in saving the empire. The election of Amcazade Köprülü Hüseyin Paşa as grand vizier in September 1697 allowed some improvements in the empire's financial situation. The progress made by the new vizier continued until he had to step down in September 1702.

Following Amcazade Paşa's resignation, the empire went into dire financial straits once again. Issues of unpaid wages and taxes depleted the empire's treasury. Sultan Mustapha II had no idea of the severity of the economic and political crises as he spent most of his time in Edirne. By July 1703, a rebellion forced the Ottoman army to abandon their king and take sides with the rebels, which led Mustapha to abdicate the throne to his brother Ahmed III (1703-1730).

During Ahmed's reign, the Ottomans kept a low profile for a while, buying enough time to reorganize their military and decrease state expenses. In 1716, the Ottomans lost to the Hapsburgs in the siege of Corfu, which lasted from July 19 to August 20, 1716. The confrontation led to the collapse of the Ottoman army following their defeat at Petrovaradin. After that, the Ottomans lost Temeş to Eugene of Savoy, Prince of the Habsburg monarchy, and they also lost Belgrade in August 1717. This devastating loss led to the signing of the treaty of Passarowitz in July 1718. This peace treaty involved the Ottomans and the Habsburgs.

The Tulip Era (Lale Devri) was a brief period of peace during which the Ottomans began to align themselves with Europe. Disasters in Iran and Ottoman interference in their matters brought the Tulip Era to an abrupt end.

Ahmed III was intellectual and had a sharp mind. He spent a lot of his time writing verse, Islamic theology, and philosophy. He was also an accomplished calligrapher like many sultans before him. The Sultan had cordial relations with France despite the terrifying nature of the Russian Empire.

Ahmed III offered his kingdom as a safe place to Charles XII of Sweden following his defeat at the hands of the Russian monarch, Peter I, at the battle of Poltava in 1709. In 1710, Charles XII convinced the Sultan to declare war on Russia. The Ottoman army, under the leadership of Baltacı Mehmet Paşa (grand vizier of the Ottoman Empire from 1704 to 1706), emerged victors at Prut's battle, also known as the Russo-Ottoman war of 1710 to 1711. This victory forced the Russians to return Azov to the Ottomans, tear down the Taganrog fortress, and cease to interfere in matters regarding the Polish-Lithuanian commonwealth.

With the help of his grand vizier Nevşehirli Damat İbrahim Pasha, Sultan Ahmed came closest to taking power from the Russians. If the Ottomans had wished it, they could have invaded Russia, expanding the Ottoman Empire all the way to Moscow. As a result of the luxuries the Sultan and his officials indulged in, he quickly became a target for the Janissaries, who, instigated by the Albanian named Patrona Halil, started a series of riots on September 20, 1730. These riots led to the Sultan's deposition in favor of his nephew, Mahmud I.

By the 19th century, the western idea of civilization led to the breakdown of the Ottoman millet.

The millet was a system of government founded by Osman I and prevalent since the beginning of the empire. The millet's dissolution led to Greek independence in 1821, Serbian independence in 1835, and Bulgarian independence between 1877 and 1878. As if this was not enough, the Ottoman public debt (dating back to August 24, 1855), which came about as a result of sultans obtaining loans from Europe during the Crimean war, had gotten to a staggering £200,000,000 with yearly interests and amortization of £12,000,000,000. The public debt was another tool used by the Europeans to control the empire politically.

The Berlin Congress of June 1878 was a crossroads in the history of southeastern Europe and the Ottoman Empire. At the end of the congress in July, Ottomans seized to be the seat of power in the Balkans. The empire lost approximately 8% of their lands and about five million of its population. The majority of the defectors were Christians, while many Muslim fugitives from the Caucasus and the Balkans fled further into the empire.

Dissolving the millets into smaller independent states made them power-hungry and set the stage for intense rivalries. The complete disintegration of the empire began between 1908 and 1922. In 1908, despite sultan Abdülhamid II's best efforts to preserve the empire, the Young Turks reformed the empire's political structure.

Sometime in 1911, Italy declared war on the Ottomans on September 29. The Ottoman forces were so feeble that the Italian army seized Tripoli and Cyrenaica by November 5 the same year. The Italians went further to send arms to Montenegro and, together with Albanian non-conformist groups, seized Rhodes. In 1912, the league of Balkans (Greece, Serbia, Bulgaria, and Montenegro) attacked the now disorganized Ottoman Empire even before their war with Italy ended.

Following the Bâb-i Âlî Baskini or the 1913 Ottoman coup headed by Ismail Enver Bey and Muhammad Talaat Bey, members of the Committee of Union and Progress (CUP) subdued the Ottomans. The treaties of London (signed May 30, 1913) and Bucharest (signed August 10, 1913) contributed to the empire losing their hold on Europe. Cities like Macedonia, Thrace, and Kosovo were lost to Ottoman allies, and Albania gained its independence.

In the reign of Mehmed V Reşâd (1844-1918), the Ottomans landed a surprise attack on Russia's Black Sea shorelines on October 29 1914. The Ottoman attack forced Russia to retaliate by allying with the British and the French to attack the Ottomans in November 1914.

The armistice of Mudros signed in October 1918 ended the war between the Ottomans, the Russians, and their allies. It also ended Ottoman involvement in the first world war. By the time Mehmed VI (1918-1922) became the Sultan, the division of the empire had led to its total integration into the world economy.

On April 22 1920, Turkish nationals gathered at the Grand National Assembly, Ankara, deep in the heart of central Anatolia. At the conference, Mustapha Kemal was elected president. This appointment began the start of an alternative government.

Mustapha Kemal's election started a brief but brutal civil war that ended with the treaty of Sèvres. This treaty eliminated whatever shreds remained of the Ottoman Empire and Turkish sovereignties. The strict terms within the Sèvres treaty removed whatever shreds left of the Ottoman Empire.

"Ottomanism" became a term that had lost its dignity. The Turkish war of independence ended with Turkish citizens seizing Anatolia.

On November 2, 1922, the Turkish government declared the abolition of the Ottoman Empire. Sultan Mehmed VI also went into exile on November 17, that same year. Sultan Abdülmecīd-i s̱ānī, also known as Abdulmejid II, was the last Sultan of the Ottoman dynasty. He was born in Dolmabahçe Palace, Beşiktaş, Istanbul, and was the cousin to his predecessor, Sultan Mehmed VI. After the exile of his cousin, he was elected by the Turkish National Assembly at Ankara. The last Sultan ruled from 1922 to 1924.

Sultan Abdülmecīd-i s̱ānī was conferred the title of a general in the Ottoman army regardless of his lack of military talent. He was more artistically inclined and played a significant part in the Ottoman artist's society. He was an accomplished artist himself and one of the most important painters of late Ottoman art. Some of his art has been displayed at a 1918 exhibition of Ottoman paintings in Vienna. His self-portrait hangs in the Pera Museum of modern art in Istanbul. He was a dedicated collector of butterflies, a hobby he engaged in for the last twenty years of his life.

In Abdulmejid II's reign, the allies and Turks convened in Lausanne, Switzerland. There, they proceeded to sign the treaty of Lausanne on July 24, 1923. Turkey was declared a republic on October 29 the same year. On April 23, 1924, the Turkish government exiled 150 high ranking Ottoman officials, including the Sultan. They were declared persona non grata for a while until the ban was lifted on June 28, 1938.

# Conclusion

The Ottoman Empire was powerful, yet flawed in many ways. Rulers of the 17th and 18th centuries were either careless, wasteful, or inexperienced. Tax problems crippled the economy leading to inflation and poverty. At a point, taxes were so steep, a lot of employees were laid off. Well-to-do Muslims were purchasing manufactured items from the Christians, leading to the influx of substandard goods from the Americas, the Far East, and India. With sultans that had become insensitive to the plight of their people, poverty became the norm. There was little or nothing left for the empire to export.

Trade decline ultimately led to a lack of revenue for the state and a drop in the gold supply. By the beginning of the 18th century, the empire had weakened at its seams, which brought about the deterioration of the Ottoman armed forces.

The 19th century brought about a boom in commerce and revenue not only because of the reforms put in place, but also because of the empire's strategic position at a junction between Europe, Asia, and Africa. Cities like Bursa and Istanbul produced the most revenue. At the height of commercial success, the Ottomans were famous for trading a lot of things. The most popular were gold, silk, dyes like indigo, porcelain from China, musk, rhubarb, and other materials.

All in all, in their golden ages, the Ottomans enjoyed success for a lot of reasons. The monarch system of government ensured that power stayed within a particular family and was not decentralized or divided between princes. This centralization of power ensured the continued success of an empire that was further cemented by Islamic belief and a state-run judicial system.

Despite their military might, the Ottomans fostered loyalty and were tolerant of other religious groups. Allowances made from these helped them out in some otherwise sticky situations in history. Power-hungry European nations also caused the decline of the empire, besides the taxation problems and lack of commerce with a desire to expand.

The development of alternative, yet just as powerful trade routes, such as the Suez Canal in Egypt, an artificial sea-level waterway constructed by a company of the same name, connecting the Mediterranean to the Red Sea, was an example of such a route. The canal, built-in 1859, led to Egypt's independence from the empire.

A decrease in agricultural productivity stemmed from the fact that the Ottoman Empire had vast lands yet remained poor in terms of capital and labor. The Ottoman market that was indispensable to European countries in the 15th and 16th centuries for cotton, wool, gold, and raw silk had become somewhat insignificant. Increased military expenditure, despite the sky-high poverty rates, increased foreign debt which spanned from 1854 to 1876, and the necessity of such liabilities made the empire a puppet in the hands of the Europeans. The debt, together with the negligence and overindulgence of some of the weaker-willed sultans, caused absolute Ottoman power to dwindle and officially fall.

Hopefully you enjoyed this book and the fascinating history of the Ottoman Empire!

History Titans

Printed in the USA
CPSIA information can be obtained
at www.ICGtesting.com
LVHW011522180224
772161LV00011B/587

9 780648 934400